SO TALL WITHIN

SOJOURNER TRUTH'S LONG WALK TOWARD FREEDOM

GARY D. SCHMIDT   ILLUSTRATED BY DANIEL MINTER

ROARING BROOK PRESS New York

In
Slavery
Time,
when
Hope
was a
seed
waiting
to be
planted

Isabella lived in a cellar where the windows never let the sun in and the floorboards never kept the water out. She had ten or twelve brothers and sisters—she couldn't be sure, since almost all of them were sold as slaves before she was old enough to remember.

But Mau-mau Bett, her mother, kept them in memory. Sometimes at night, she held Isabella and pointed to the skies over New York State. "Those are the same stars, and that is the same moon, that look down upon your brothers and sisters," she whispered. And Isabella looked at those same stars, that same moon, and dreamed.

When Isabella was about nine, she was sold for a hundred dollars—along with a flock of sheep. Mau-mau Bett held her one last time. They would always remember to look at those same stars and that same moon, even though they would be "ever so far away from . . . each other."

Every night after that, Isabella kept her eyes wide open.

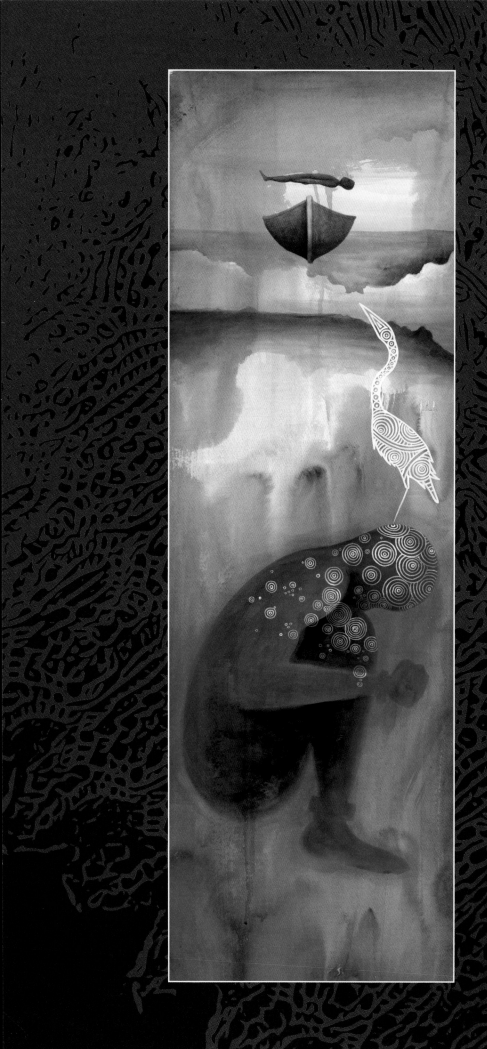

In
Slavery
Time,
when
Happiness
was a
dream
never
coming
true,

Isabella was put to work. "Now the war begun," she thought.

First she worked for Mr. Nealy, who figured she didn't need shoes in wintertime.

Two years later, she worked for Mr. Schryver, who had her carry fish and hoe corn and dig roots and tend herbs and tote gallons of dark molasses.

A year and a half after that, she worked for Mr. Dumont, who bragged that Isabella could "do a good family's washing in the night, and be ready in the morning to go into the field." And she did, night after night, day after day, night after night, day after day, night after night, day after day.

But sometimes she looked up at those stars and that moon,
and she asked God "if He thought it was right."

In
Slavery
Time,
when
Respect
fell as
often as
snow
in July,

Mr. Dumont ordered Isabella to marry a slave named Thomas. She had five children—James, who died in infancy, Diana, Peter, Elizabeth, and Sophia.

At night, under the light of those stars and that moon, she wondered if her children and her children's children would always be slaves too.

In
Slavery
Time,
when
Promises
were
thin
as old
smoke,

Mr. Dumont swore that "if she would do well," he would free Isabella and give her a log cabin to live in by the next summer—a year before all the slaves in New York State had to be freed by law.

But the summer came and the summer passed. "Oh," thought Isabella, "I have felt as if I could not live."

So that fall, after the work of the harvest was done, she held baby Sophia close and seized Freedom with her own hands.

Along the road, she came to the house of Isaac and Maria Van Wagener. They welcomed her inside. They promised they would never abandon her. They were there when Mr. Dumont found Isabella.

"You've run away from me," said Mr. Dumont.

"No," said Isabella. "I walked away by daylight."

"You must go back," he said.

Isabella shook her head.

"I shall take the child," said Mr. Dumont.

But Isaac and Maria kept their promise. They paid
Mr. Dumont's price for all the work Isabella might have done before
she was freed by law, and they paid his price for her baby, and Mr. Dumont left.

Isabella asked Isaac and Maria if they were her new masters.

Isaac shook his head. He was master to no one, he said.

And now Isabella was slave to no one.

But in
Slavery
Time,
Broken
Promises
were like
leaves on
a tree.

Mr. Dumont sold Isabella's five-year-old son, Peter, to Mr. Gedney, who sent him down South. Though Isabella could not read or write, she knew that in New York, where they lived, no slave could be sold outside the state's borders.

Isabella, on foot and alone, went to the Dumont house and knocked on the door. Hard. And when it opened, she said, "I'll have my child!"

Mrs. Dumont shook her head. "A fine fuss to make!" she said, and closed the door.

So Isabella walked to the Gedney house and knocked on the door. "I must have my child!"

Mrs. Gedney told her that Peter had gone to live with her married daughter, "to have enough of everything, and be treated like a gentleman."

But Isabella knew this was a lie. "My boy has gone as a slave, and he is too little to go so far from his mother," she said.

Mrs. Gedney closed the door.

But Isabella thought, "I felt so tall within—I felt as if the power of a nation was with me!"

Isabella traveled miles and miles across New York to Kingston to tell her story to the Grand Jury. They saw how tall within she was. They gave her a letter for the sheriff, demanding that Peter be brought home. She took the letter and walked miles and miles back.

Peter was already far away in Alabama, but Mr. Gedney read the letter and knew he must obey the court. He went down South to find Peter, while Isabella waited and prayed: "God, help me get my son. If you were in trouble, as I am, and I could help you, as you can me, think I wouldn't do it?"

After a few months, Isabella held Peter again. But the Alabama masters had whipped Peter, and kicked him, and beaten him. He would never really heal.

That was Slavery.

In
Slavery
Time,
when
Chains tore
families
apart like
the wind
frays a
flag,

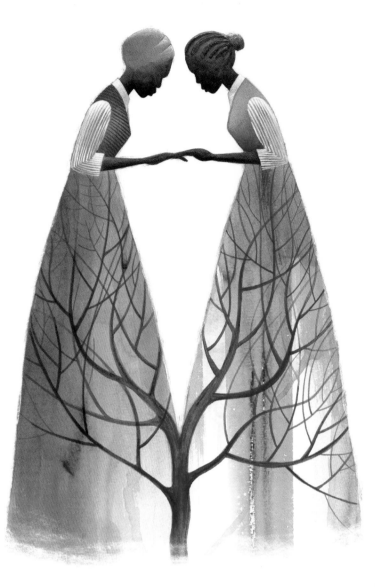

Isabella still looked up at those stars and that moon and hoped her brothers and sisters saw them too.

They did.

A year after Peter was freed, he and Isabella moved to New York City, where she met a woman named Nancy at Zion's Church. When they held hands, Isabella said, "the bony hardness [was] so just like mine." But Nancy passed away.

Soon afterward she met her sister Sophia, and then her brother Michael, who had been stolen from her long ago. They told her they'd had another sister in the city, but she had just died. Her name had been Nancy.

Then Isabella understood that one of the first people she had met in New York City was her own sister—but she had not known it.

"What is this slavery," wondered Isabella, "that it can do such dreadful things?"

Perhaps that was the moment Isabella knew she had a journey to make under those stars and that moon. It would be a journey—a *sojourn*—to tell the truth about Slavery. And maybe then, Slavery would end forever.

More than fifteen years after she walked away from the Dumonts, Isabella changed her name to Sojourner Truth, and she began to walk again.

In
Slavery
Time,
when
Words
seemed
weaker
than
whips,

Sojourner Truth left New York City with a bundle of clothing on one arm and a basket of food on the other. She began to speak out against Slavery to whoever would listen.

Not everyone wanted to hear, but she had "the lever of truth."

So she spoke.

In Massachusetts she said, "What a beautiful world this would be, when we should see everything right side up."

In Ohio she said that she had seen some of her children "sold off into slavery, and when I cried out with a mother's grief, none but Jesus heard."

In Indiana she said, "The truth is powerful and will prevail."

In
Slavery
Time,
when
Tiredness
stood
at the
doorway,

Sojourner Truth walked all the way to Washington, D.C. There she met Abraham Lincoln, and she told him he was "the best president who has ever taken the seat."

In Michigan she collected food and clothing for the Black regiments of free men and former slaves fighting in the Civil War to end Slavery.

In Virginia she worked with the Freedmen's Bureau to teach liberated slaves how to live in Freedom. When some people wanted to stop her, she warned that if they tried, she "would rock the United States like a cradle."

And in Washington, D.C., when a streetcar conductor would not pull up for her, she cried, "I want to ride!" so loudly that the carriage traffic around them stopped, and she got on. The conductor threatened to throw her off, but she told him that she "knew the laws as well as he did," and she stayed on and rode longer than she had planned—"to make the most of it."

For years and years, Sojourner Truth walked and told her story and fought for Freedom. And when Slavery Time finally ended, she felt so tall within.

In
Freedom
Time,
when Hope
kindled a
fire in the
dark and
Happiness
winked
over the
horizon,

Sojourner Truth told an audience in Massachusetts, "Children, I have come here like the rest of you, to hear what I have to say." And what she had to say was plenty. She spoke of a woman's right to vote. She spoke about making prisons more humane. She asked the government to offer land to former slaves. She spoke against capital punishment. For almost fifteen more years, she walked thousands of miles—to Philadelphia and to Brooklyn and to Washington, D.C. And to Kansas and Iowa and Missouri and Wisconsin and Illinois and all over Michigan. And everywhere she went, she spoke of Freedom.

In
Freedom
Time,
when
Respect
wanted to
show its
face and
Broken
Promises
tried to
mend,

Sojourner Truth walked to Battle Creek, Michigan, where she lived with her free daughters and free grandchildren. And Sojourner Truth was weary, and ready to lay down her lever.

In
Freedom
Time,
when
Chains
broke
and Words
got up to
sing and
Tiredness,
oh Tiredness,
danced a
Hallelujah,

Sojourner Truth asked herself, What is anybody in the world for?

Then she looked up at those same stars, that same moon, and she saw them shining over everyone. Over everyone!

And she knew what she had been in the world for.

"[I] had a work to do," she thought. "My lost time that I lost being a slave was made up."

BIOGRAPHICAL NOTE

In the fall of 2014, *Smithsonian* magazine named Sojourner Truth one of the "100 Most Significant Americans of All Time." She appears in the category "First Women," but she could have appeared in "Trailblazers," or "Rebels and Resisters," or "Religious Figures," or even, given the miles she covered with her walking, in "Athletes." But whatever category one chooses, we see her now as part of a great national heritage, one of those few figures who have defined our sense of who we are as Americans.

She probably would have been surprised to be included.

In about 1797, she was born into slavery in Ulster County, New York, as Isabella Baumfree. The family that called her their slave was Dutch, and this was the language she spoke until she was sold to the Nealy family in 1806. That was when she began to learn English—since the Nealys needed her to understand their commands. Several years later, she was sold to the Dumont family, with whom she lived for sixteen years, until Mr. Dumont broke his promise to free her a year before she would have been emancipated by state law. Her anger at this betrayal led her to flee her enslavement, and, aided by the Van Wageners, she did indeed break away from the Dumonts—an astonishing accomplishment!

But that was only the beginning of her astonishing accomplishments. When her son Peter was illegally sold out of New York State, Isabella successfully sued to have him returned. Tragically, Peter had been savagely beaten and so brainwashed that he clung to his oppressors and was fearful of his own mother. Though he did finally acknowledge her, perhaps he never fully recovered from the separation and the humiliations he had suffered; after he and his mother moved to New York City, he eventually began what Isabella would describe as "a low and worthless" life. He later went to sea to avoid trouble with the law. After several letters—the last in 1841—she never heard from him again. The death of Peter may have reminded her powerfully of the loss of her other son, James, who died in infancy, and of her long separation from Diana, who stayed with the Dumonts and lived in New York. Sometime after 1849, Diana moved west to Michigan, and her sisters joined her in houses owned by Sojourner Truth in Harmonia and Battle Creek. Elizabeth had two children, the oldest of whom—Samuel Banks—traveled with Sojourner Truth in the 1870s. Sophia married Thomas Schuyler and had three children, the oldest of whom they named Sojourner.

It may have been this loss of Peter, or perhaps her sister Nancy's death, or perhaps a religious experience that led Isabella to change her name to Sojourner Truth in 1843 and begin to walk around the country, proclaiming God's truth: "Children, I talk to God and God talks to me." She became one of the country's more popular guests at camp meetings and associations, where she spoke of religious revival, and—before and during the Civil War—about the abolition of slavery. After the Civil War, she spoke about the rights of women and the rights of the newly freed African Americans, who deserved roles in the national life that reflected their liberty. Her moral courage and powerfully ethical voice helped to put Americans on a journey to a new and larger understanding of the essential and vital equality of all the country's citizens.

Her story was first published in her *Narrative of Sojourner Truth* in 1850. The *Narrative* was republished in 1878, adding selections from her *Book of Life*, which collected letters and tales of her efforts to promote the equality of all people. The book documents Sojourner Truth's stubbornly-held belief that her efforts might someday bring real change. In one story she recorded, a man came up to her after she had spoken at a meeting.

> "Old woman, do you think that your talk about slavery does any good? Do you suppose people care what you say? . . . I don't care any more for your talk than I do for the bite of a flea."
>
> "Perhaps not," she responded, "but, the Lord willing, I'll keep you scratching."

Sojourner Truth kept Americans scratching until she died in 1883, in Battle Creek, Michigan, where she had been living with her daughters and their families.

She still keeps Americans scratching.

BIBLIOGRAPHY

The most important book we have about Sojourner Truth is the one in which we get closest to her own voice: *Narrative of Sojourner Truth*. The book was first published in Boston in 1850, and then reprinted in 1878 in Battle Creek, Michigan, adding her *Book of Life* to the original *Narrative*. (This 1878 edition is the source of all quotations in *So Tall Within*.) A facsimile reprint of this edition was published in 1991 by Oxford University Press as part of the Schomburg Library of Nineteenth-Century Black Women Writers series. A digital version of the original 1850 *Narrative* is available at digital.library.upenn.edu/women /truth/1850/1850.html.

But—and this is a big "but"—Sojourner Truth dictated her story to Olive Gilbert, a white abolitionist, and in 1850, Olive Gilbert was listed as the author of the *Narrative*. We can never know how authentic the words we hear from these pages are, and how much of it is Gilbert's version of Sojourner Truth's own compelling voice.

While *So Tall Within* tells a story of Sojourner Truth's struggle against slavery in America, many other books chronicle her moral struggles for civil rights, for women's rights, and for temperance. These include Jacqueline Bernard, *Journey Toward Freedom: The Story of Sojourner Truth* (New York: Feminist Press, 1990); Erlene Stetson and Linda David, *Glorying in Tribulation: The Lifework of Sojourner Truth* (East Lansing: Michigan State University Press, 1994); Suzanne Pullon Fitch and Roseann M. Mandziuk, *Sojourner Truth as Orator: Wit, Story, and Song* (Westport, Conn.: Greenwood Press, 1997); Jennifer Blizin Gillis, *Sojourner Truth* (Chicago: Heinemann Library, 2006); Carleton Mabee and Susan Mabee Newhouse, *Sojourner Truth—Slave, Prophet, Legend* (New York: New York University Press, 1993); Nell Irvin Painter, *Sojourner Truth: A Life, a Symbol* (New York: W.W. Norton, 1996)—Painter also wrote an introduction for the *Narrative of Sojourner Truth* for Penguin Books in 1998—and Margaret Washington, *Sojourner Truth's America* (Urbana: University of Illinois Press, 2009).

Episode One, "There Is a River," of the PBS documentary *This Far by Faith* recounts the life of Sojourner Truth and explores the ways in which her religious faith informed her struggle against the institution of slavery (pbs.org/thisfarbyfaith/people /sojourner_truth.html). Her famous "Ar'n't I a Woman?" speech, delivered in 1851 at the Women's Rights Convention in Akron, Ohio, is recreated by Kerry Washington in a video available at history.com/topics/holidays/womens-history-month/videos/aint -i-a-woman. Here, again, however, the voice of Sojourner Truth comes from the transcription of a white woman, Frances Gage, who organized the conference and probably inserted the title line and the southern dialect that many have ascribed to Sojourner Truth—who grew up speaking Dutch.

Younger readers might wish to consult Peter Krass, *Sojourner Truth: Antislavery Activist* (New York: Chelsea House, 1988); Yona Zeldis McDonough, *Who Was Sojourner Truth?* (New York: Grosset & Dunlap, 2015); Patricia and Frederick McKissack, *Sojourner Truth: A Voice for Freedom* (Berkeley Heights, N.J.: Enslow Publishers, 2002); Andrea Davis Pinkney, *Sojourner Truth's Step-Stomp Stride* (New York: Disney/Jump at the Sun Books, 2009), illustrated by Brian Pinkney; Anne Rockwell, *Only Passing Through: The Story of Sojourner Truth* (New York: Alfred A. Knopf, 2000), illustrated by R. Gregory Christie; Peter and Connie Roop, *Sojourner Truth* (New York: Scholastic, 2002); and Ann Turner, *My Name Is Truth: The Life of Sojourner Truth* (New York: Harper, 2015), illustrated by James Ransome.

ARTIST'S NOTE

When I sat down to illustrate *So Tall Within*, I approached the text as a work of poetry. It conjured feelings that allowed me to view the narrative of Sojourner Truth in a contemporary light. Inspired by this poetic reading, I created a series of vertical paintings that are loosely planted in the times of legal slavery but that parallel the feeling of struggle in today's streets—the feeling that you may be buried, but you are surrounded by soil that nourishes you.

One panel has an image of a young man in a slave collar, a bizarre accoutrement used to prevent people from running away. For me, this nineteenth-century image has echoes in present times. This individual prison of metal and chains has now evolved into prison data records and religious and racial profiling that follow an individual, limiting his or her access to citizenship and free movement.

The story of Sojourner Truth shows the value of deep inner strength even when others try to deny your humanity. It shows the power of spirituality, self-worth, and the determination to live a right life in a wrong world. I believe that when Isabella told the painful details of her life and struggles, it was her way of sharing her strength and psychic armor with us so that we could continue the walk long after she laid her lever down.

For Ashley Bryan, with gratitude for a long friendship —*G.D.S.*

To my Eight Tall Sisters, whose strength and embrace I always rely on —*D.M.*

Text copyright © 2018 by Gary D. Schmidt
Illustrations copyright © 2018 by Daniel Minter

Published by Roaring Brook Press
Roaring Brook Press is a division of Holtzbrinck Publishing Holdings Limited Partnership
175 Fifth Avenue, New York, NY 10010

mackids.com

Library of Congress Control Number: 2018932819

ISBN: 9781626728721

Our books may be purchased in bulk for promotional, educational, or business use. Please contact
your local bookseller or the Macmillan Corporate and Premium Sales Department at (800) 221-7945 ext. 5442
or by e-mail at MacmillanSpecialMarkets@macmillan.com.

First edition, 2018
Printed in China by RR Donnelley Asia Printing Solutions Ltd.,
Dongguan City, Guangdong Province

1 3 5 7 9 10 8 6 4 2